IMAGES OF ENGLAND

AROUND BODMIN

IMAGES OF ENGLAND

AROUND BODMIN

JOHN NEALE

For Keith Weary, a friend, who is proud to be 'a son of Bodmin', and for Bodmin people everywhere.

Frontispiece: This picture shows a china model of a Roman jug inscribed 'Bodmin' on a Trent Bridge postcard, which was mailed from Bodmin on 12 August 1906. Collin Brewer collection

First published in 2003 by Tempus Publishing

Reprinted in 2009 by
The History Press
The Mill, Brimscombe Port,
Stroud, Gloucestershire, GL5 2QG
www.thehistorypress.co.uk

Reprinted 2011, 2012, 2013

© John Neale, 2011

The right of John Neale to be identified as the Author of this work has been asserted in accordance with the Copyrights, Designs and Patents Act 1988.

All rights reserved. No part of this book may be reprinted or reproduced or utilised in any form or by any electronic, mechanical or other means, now known or hereafter invented, including photocopying and recording, or in any information storage or retrieval system, without the permission in writing from the Publishers.

British Library Cataloguing in Publication Data.
A catalogue record for this book is available from the British Library.

ISBN 978 07524 3054 6

Typesetting and origination by
Tempus Publishing Limited.
Printed in Great Britain.

Contents

	Acknowledgements	7
	Introduction	9
one	In and around Bodmin: the county town	10
two	Bodmin people	47
three	Bodmin through war to peace	77
four	Tredethy, Pencarrow, Lanivet, St Mabyn and Blisland	91
five	Lanhydrock, Respryn and Carminnow Cross	99
six	Altarnun, Five Lanes, Trewint and North Hill	103
seven	Bolventor, Jamaica Inn, Dozmary Pool and Davidstow	117
eight	Cardinham, St Neot and St Cleer	123

Acknowledgements

I should like to thank the following people and organisations for providing information for this book and for giving me free access to their photographic collections:

Mrs Maureen Tooze (Curator), Dr and Mrs Johnson, Miss Corinne Norton, Mr R Sheppard, Mrs Doreen Luke and all the welcoming faces at Bodmin Town Museum. Lady Molesworth St Aubyn, Pencarrow (and Mr James Reynolds, Administrator); Mr Terry Knight and staff at the Cornwall Centre, Redruth; the staff of Cornwall County Library, Bodmin, for use of their photographic collection; Mrs Sue Parker, Manager, Cornwall County Library, Launceston, for access to her family photographs and for help in the identification of those people in other pictures.

The staff of Cornwall County Library, Launceston; Amanda Sutherland, Museum Officer; Devon and Cornwall Police, Exeter. Mr Collin Brewer, who trusted me with rare and valuable pictures from his personal collection. Bodmin Photographers: Alan Date; Richard, Baron Hony; George Ellis; Halcliff Studio; A.J.F. Bond; Hawken, Heygate and Son; Clemens Photography; Charles Woolf, Newquay, John Rapson and David Hambly, Liskeard. The files of the Cornish Guardian, Bodmin; Cornish and Devon Post, Launceston; and the Cornish Times, Liskeard.

Special thanks are due to all those authors whose books and papers on Bodmin and district have contained 'signposts' in their pages, and as always to Overland, Photo Precision Ltd of St Albans, Valentine's Argyll, Frith, Woolstone, Judges and all the other anonymous postcard publishers and photographers. Mrs Ruth Hobbs, Keith Weary, Trevor Scantlebury, Douglas Lewis, Robert Tremain, Wilfred Hoskin, Andrew Langdon, Ian Parnall, Gerald and Audrey Fry, Mr Keith Searle, Keith Truscott, Mr Ivor Whiting, Mr Frank Grigg, Mrs Gloria Hooper, Mrs M. Bunney, Mr John Pagram, Bude, Roy and Dorothy Neale, Arthur and Barbara Masters. Also, all those in Bodmin who have provided obscure facts and snippets of information. Thank you one and all.

Lastly, I offer my thanks and deepest apologies to anyone whom I have inadvertently overlooked.

Introduction

When I was asked, out of the blue, to compile this book about Bodmin, I hesitated for two reasons. Firstly, I felt it would be too much of a challenge; and secondly, there is no way for me that Bodmin can be separated from its moor, so this is an effort to combine the two in text and photographs.

This book is in no way an attempt to write, or even scratch the surface of, the long and proud history of Bodmin. That has been written with great scholarship and detail by people who are far better qualified than I to do so.

Bodmin has been 'on the map' since earliest times. By the time the Saxons made their presence felt the settlement was already important in religious affairs. Later the Priory, one of the biggest in the county, was established, and a succession of priors ruled Bodmin, doing very much as they pleased, until the Dissolution in 1539. Over the decades various charters were granted conferring priviledges on Bodmin and gradually the good people of the town had more say in day-to-day events and affairs.

Slowly Bodmin grew in importance. The County Lunatic Asylum was established and, due to the town's more central position, the County Assizes were transferred to Bodmin from Launceston. The County Gaol was built in Bodmin and in 1877 the Duke of Cornwall's Light Infantry Regimental Depot was established there. Bodmin consequently gained further status and was recognised as the County Town. Despite all these advances at Bodmin, Launceston remained the capital of Cornwall, a status granted by Charter from Philip and Mary in 1553, a document which has never been recinded.

At one time it was proposed to build the cathedral for the newly formed Anglican Diocese of Cornwall in Bodmin but, in the event, like several other places – St Columb, Helston, Lostwithiel and Launceston among them – Bodmin lost out to Truro.

Almost every facet of history has touched Bodmin in one way or another and the town has taken centre stage in both county affairs and in times of national crisis. During the Second World War Bodmin was at the centre of military affairs in the region. Thousands of troops were stationed in the town, a fact not overlooked by the Germans in August 1942, when two German bombers bombed the town.

Bodmin means different things to different people. To some it has always been 'home'. To older people who have moved away, Bodmin means a pleasant place to retire among friends and relatives when they can no longer resist the pull of old family ties. Younger people find that it means regular employment at one or other of the town's several industrial estates, business parks or out-of-town superstores. Criticise Bodmin or compare it unfavourably with any other Cornish town in front of anyone who is Bodmin born and bred and you will quickly discover exactly how strong their loyalty can be.

Bodmin has changed over the years: the Southern Railway, the Great Western Railway and the Duke of Cornwall's Light Infantry Depot have all come and gone. Since its closure the Southern Railway station has been obliterated from the townscape by new developments; there is now only a small military presence based at the Military Museum in Bodmin.

Other buildings in the town have disappeared. Quiller Couch's house was torn down in 1970; the Globe Inn, later the Duke of Cornwall in Church Square, and cottages in Dennison Road, Downing Square and Downing Street were demolished to make way for the Finn VC estate. The Church of England School in Robartes Road was torn down to be replaced by Bederkesa Court. The site of the Congregational Chapel in Fore Street is now occupied by the Job Centre, and the site of the cinema is today a Building Society. Small shops around the town have closed and been converted into accommodation; other stores have succumbed to the pressure of joining their bigger brothers on the outskirts. Tenby House on Dennison Road was demolished to make way for the Somerfield access road. Perhaps one of the most significant changes was 'overspill', when families from many distant places came to live in Bodmin, causing the town's population to soar.

There are as many 'Bodmins' as there are people living there. Everyone can recall a favourite character, a memory or an incident, or has a tale to tell about the town of yesterday.

Bodmin is so steeped in age-old history that it is impossible to cover every aspect of its colourful past in a book such as this, so the content is very much a matter of personal choice. I hope I have resurrected, in pictures and text, memories of Bodmin and its moor in days now gone – of those dear relatives, friends and neighbours whom we loved in their time, when life was slower and everyone knew everyone else as they walked the streets about their daily business, or beat the bounds, sang in choirs, fought fires, put on theatrical productions, played sports or tramped the moor to Roughtor, Kilmar and Brown Willy. It is these people whose likenesses make up the cast of these few pages, who in their different ways forged Bodmin and its moor into what it is today.

Hopefully this book will please those who know Bodmin. I readily confess to knowing more about the town now than I did at the outset, and to thoroughly enjoying the learning curve. If this small volume does nothing more than encourage one reader to save an old photograph of Bodmin, to remember a name or a small snippet of information which will link other seemingly insignificant pieces together, then it will have served its purpose and I shall be well pleased.

John Neale
Launceston, 2003

one

In and around Bodmin: The County Town

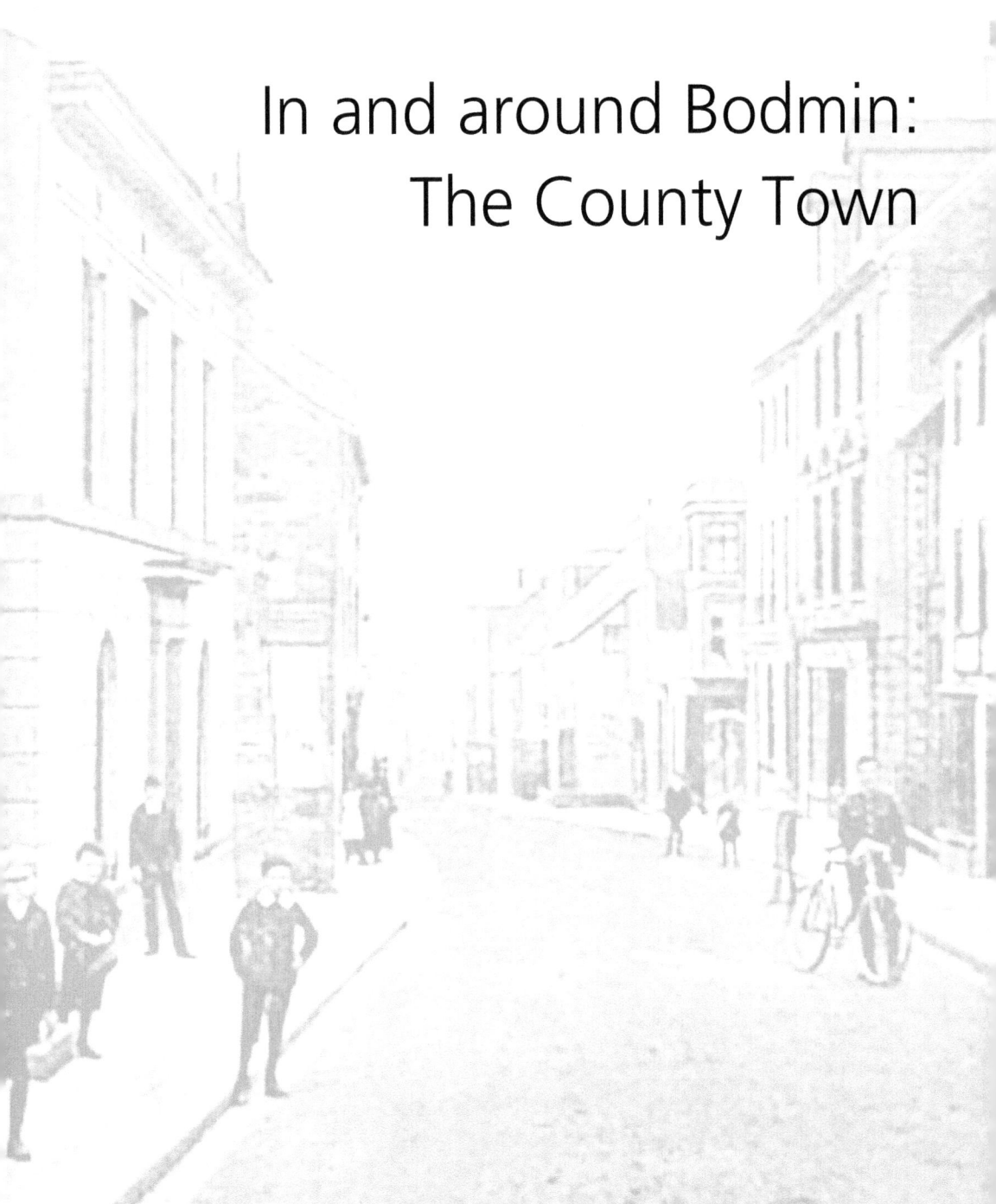

Like most other Cornish towns, Bodmin has undergone many changes in the last few decades. Fore street and Lower and Higher Bore streets, with their varying architectural styles, being the heart of the town, are no exception. Beautiful buildings have been demolished, generations old shop fronts have changed and others have come and gone, often in a matter of months. Motor vehicles have demanded road-widening schemes and changes in general street furniture. The side streets and other parts of the town have not escaped change. Both major and more subtle developments have taken place, each in its turn making an alteration to the overall streetscape. This section shows some of the street scenes of yesterday and adaptations that have taken place.

Above left: St Petroc, a Welsh prince, who trained in Ireland, took over the running of the early Christian community which had been established in Bodmin and made it the 'Abode of the Monks', soon recognised as the main religious centre of the west. He established the Priory and died in AD 564.

Above right: The stately rows of beech trees which once bordered Priory Avenue, the entrance road to the town from the Liskeard direction, were felled in a road-widening scheme. At least one Bodmin resident still describes the loss as an absolute tragedy.

Aerial view of Bodmin showing the Assize Court. The square building in the centre of the picture is the cinema at the bottom of Fore Street.

Stooks of corn, a long-gone country sight, and the field patterns stretching toward the Beacon. The granite Gilbert Memorial obelisk, soaring to 114 feet on the horizon catches the eye on the approach to Bodmin from every direction.

Above: View over the roof tops of Bodmin from Castle Hill toward Crinnicks Hill and the 17H-acre Beacon, topped by the town's famous landmark, the Gilbert Memorial obelisk. The Beacon is now a nature reserve, established by the North Cornwall District Council and Bodmin Town Council, and opened in 1994 after a speculator expressed interest in developing the area. Trees have been planted and part of the area is being allowed to grow back into its natural state.

Left: The Gilbert Monument on the Beacon designed by Pease of Boconnoc, built by Eva of Helston and inscribed by a Bodmin mason named Buscombe was completed in 1857, at a cost of £1,500. It recognises Gilbert's exceptional service as a Divisional Commander during the Sikh Wars. In 1902, to mark the Coronation of King Edward VII, a huge bonfire costing £30 was built near the monument by the Bodmin Coronation Bonfire Committee. Among those in charge were T.H. Spear, T. Hore, R. Buscombe, G. Buscombe, W.A. Sandoe, F. Zimber and E.V. George. In 1910, a corner stone became displaced, evidently the needle had been struck by lightning. Messrs Harris contractors repositioned the stone. In 1933 the needle was thought to be swaying unduly and stone had fallen off. Thankfully the famous landmark still stands.

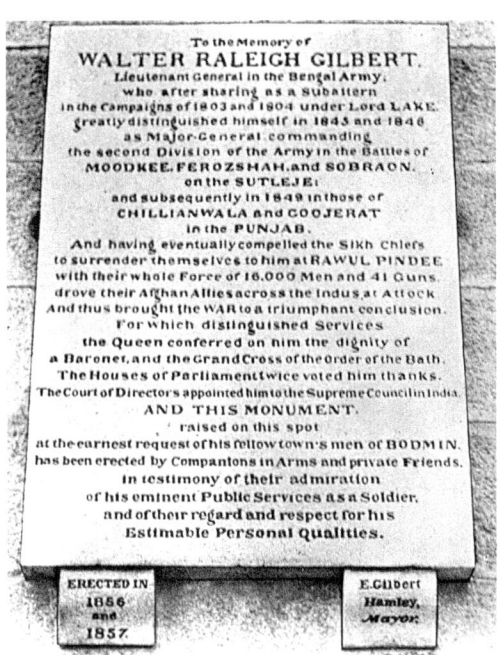

The plaque on the Gilbert monument giving details of the illustrious soldier's career.

A bleak wintry scene in Bodmin – St Petroc's Church, the largest in Cornwall, pictured here after a heavy snow fall. The church is the main focal point of religious life in the town. At one time a brewery stood opposite the church and much of the water used by the brewery came from a stream flowing from under the churchyard.

St Petroc's seen from the southwest, as it looked in the 1930s. Until the end of the seventeenth century the church sported a spire soaring to 150 feet, unfortunately it was struck by lightning and crashed, damaging the church. The spire was never rebuilt.

St Petroc's seen from the Robartes Gardens, which were opened in 1902. In August that year the Borough Council became concerned about the damage being done to the gardens by vandals. To combat this problem it was decided that a copy of the relevant by-law should be fixed in a prominent position, the granite posts were cleaned, wire baskets for rubbish were erected and wooden stakes were placed around each tree.

A glimpse of the interior of St Petroc's. By the time this picture was taken in 1934 the choir stalls and organ had been moved to the west end to make way for the Duke of Cornwall's Light Infantry Chapel where the Regimental Colours were laid up in 1962.

Below left: Just peeping from behind the present reredos and altar is the Victorian stone reredos. Over the years this part of St Petroc's Church has undergone several changes.

Below right: This picture shows the tomb of Thomas Vivian, the penultimate prior of Bodmin, who died in 1533. His tomb, carved from Catacleuse stone from Harlyn Bay, shows the Vivian arms and the priory arms (three fish), as well as those of King Henry VIII. After the Reformation Prior Vivian's remains were removed from the old Priory and brought to St Petroc's Church.

St Thomas' Chapel ruins after the removal of the foliage, pictured in more recent times, showing the attractive window tracery.

St Guron's Holy Well at the west end exterior. St Guron founded the first Christian cell hereabouts in AD 500. The granite building covers his well. The earliest reference to the well appears in the twelfth century. The well house is thought to date from the early fourteenth century. At one time this was the main source of the town's water supply. The two gargoyles are dated 1545.

Above: Priory pond and house. This picture shows a view across the old priory fish pond toward the house. The pond, part of the monastic complex, was fed by a stream. The surrounding wall we see today is a more recent innovation.

Left: Entrance porch to the Georgian Priory house, built by William Pennington in the late eighteenth century on what was once monastic land. Later the house became the home of Sir Walter Raleigh Gilbert, who is commemorated on the Beacon monument. In 1928 the house was sold at the Royal Hotel to Coode and Gifford of St Austell. During the Second World War the residence became a billett for the A.T.S. Bodmin Borough Council purchased the property in the late 1940s for municipal offices. Today it is home to the Social Services Education Office.

Before the Royal Cornwall Agricultural Show found a permanent home at Wadebridge it used to travel to various locations around the county. In 1948 it visited Bodmin. This picture shows the Priory house floodlit for the occasion.

The chough is the county bird and as such is a potent symbol of Cornwall. A giant chough, made from reed and aluminium, measuring twelve feet in height and with a wingspan of ten feet, was commissioned from Sue and Peter Hill, by the Bodmin Heritage Organisation as part of the 2001 Heritage Day festivities. Afterwards the bird became a focal point on the island in the fish pond in Priory Park.

Bodmin's saddest memorial – a canine drinking trough of polished granite in the Priory Park car park – remembers two pet dogs, owned by Prince Chula Chakrabongse of Thailand, who lived at nearby Tredethy House. The memorial was presented to Bodmin by the prince in memory of Joan, a wire-haired terrier who died in 1948 aged seventeen, and Hercules, a bulldog who died in 1954.

Exterior of the building which from 1749 to 1779 was the town's Debtors' Prison, one of only three in Cornwall. The building stands in Crockwell Street, then known as Prison Lane. Later it became known as the Board Wine and Spirit Vaults. The current name, the Hole in the Wall, although harking back to its former use, dates from only the 1930s.

Interior of the Hole in the Wall public house. During the Second World War it was a favourite haunt of troops stationed in Bodmin. The old Carnewater Leat, now piped for much of its length, is still visible as it runs through the garden, to which, since its interior refurbishment, the celebrated lion which once overlooked the bar has been relegated.

Wells are woven into the history of Bodmin. The Bree Shute Well, more fondly known as The Eye Well, is located near the Dennison Road car park. Water from this well was used for bathing the eyes, the well having a reputation for healing all kinds of optical complaints. The well also supplied adequate water, once described as 'fairly good water' for daily use for domestic purposes.

Above: A part of the East Cornwall Hospital, built by W.E. Bennett in 1910. Over the years it was enlarged and through gifts and bequests was able to keep abreast of modern treatments. Sadly this much-loved facility was closed in 2002, to be replaced by a modern hospital complex of 145 beds in six blocks.

Right: The 50ft high Berry Tower dating from between 1501 and 1514 is all that remains of the church of the Holy Rood or Cross. The tower marks the position of the Monstery of Dinuurin. In the ninth century it was the seat of the Cornish Bishops. The tower was incorporated into the new cemetery in the nineteenth century. In the early 1990s the towers future was uncertain as demolition was threatened. A public outcry against the proposal ensued and the tower was saved.

The Assize Courts and mayoralty beyond, pictured in November 1905. The mayoralty was the judge's lodging when the assizes were in session. From this photograph it looks as if caps were the height of fashion for the boys.

Another view of Mount Folly Square and the Assize Court, built between 1837 and 1838 to designs by Henry Burt of Launceston. Here the fountain makes a convenient place to meet and chat. A hundred years ago a dispute erupted about the charge made for the water. Some thought the money should be spent on town improvements and not on water; others argued that a fountain without water was useless.

Above: Mount Folly pictured in former years. When visiting Bodmin, Miss Norma Smith used the area to address a large crowd, mostly ladies, to campaign on behalf of the non-militant suffragists. In 1902 Coronation souvenir mugs were presented and street parties were held on the open space. The results of elections were announced from the balcony of the public rooms in the centre of the picture.

Right: Mount Folly as it was in the 1940s. According to the writer of the postcard, the YMCA was just around the corner from where the man is standing by his bicycle. The North Cornwall Fox Hounds met here on numerous occasions.

Above: In 1988 the Crown Courts moved from Bodmin to Truro. Prior to the last sitting, a service at which the Bishop of Truro, Rt Rev. Peter Mumford officiated, was held at St Petroc's. The last judge was Mr Justice Nolan, High Court Judge for the Western Circuit. Other judges who had sat at Bodmin attended, as did Mrs Diana Colville, High Sheriff of Cornwall. Later, part of the court complex became a restaurant, then Bodmin Town Council purchased the building, since when the area has undergone an extensive makeover. The celebrated Hayward's Grill restaurant opposite has closed.

Left: The famous Turret Clock built on the site of the old Butter market stands at the junction of Fore Street, Honey Street and Crockwell Street. This edifice was erected by Captain Collins of Trewardale during the mayoralty of his nephew J.B. Collins, 1844–45.

This Clemens picture shows the frontage of the Palace Cinema which was opened as the Kinema on the junction of Fore Street, Crockwell Street and Honey Street by the Pellow family in 1921. In 1931 it became the Palace Theatre. The last manager was Mr Bauress. After closure the Palace Theatre became a bingo hall. The building was eventually pulled down in 1988.

Fore Street, Bodmin.

Above: Fore Street 1906. The Congregational chapel opened in 1870 is on the left of the picture. After demolition the site was occupied by a small supermarket. Hancock's fruit and vegetable shop stood nearby.

Opposite above: Looking down Fore Street in 1906. On the left is the Congregational Chapel, also known as Lady Huntingdon's Connexion, so called after Selina, Countess of Huntingdon. This formidable lady established numerous Connexion chapels, mostly in the south, and encouraged her chaplains to preach in them. The building was demolished in the 1960s. The modern Job Centre now stands on the site.

Opposite below: Looking down Fore Street. The Royal Hotel is on the left. Its canopy and porch were removed sometime before the hotel finally closed.

Interior of the Congregational Chapel, a feature of which was the corona. George Ellis, the celebrated Bodmin photographer, was the regular organist here for several years.

Looking up Fore Street from the Turret Clock. The Trade Mark free house is on the left, selling Allsopp's Burton Ale. Billing's Queens Head Hotel was next door. Today the premises are occupied by the Imperial Cancer Research charity shop. Brewer's high-class outfitters are nearby.

A rare view of Fore Street, showing the market building on the left and Cardell's stores on the right. The Devon and Cornwall Bank is now a branch of Lloyds TSB.

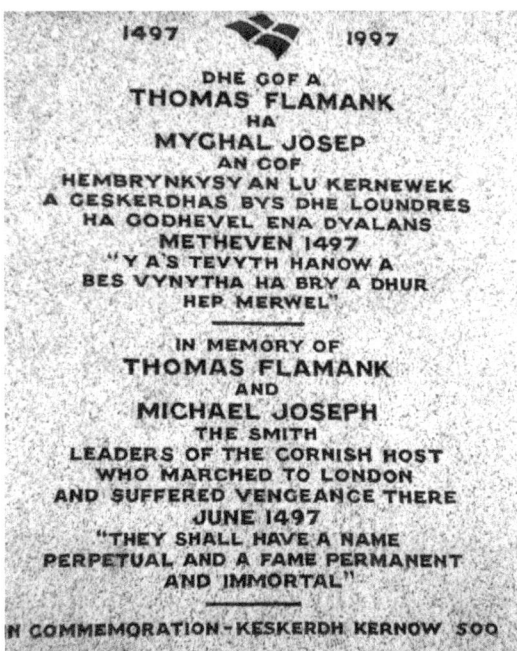

A recent addition to the Fore Street scene is the Thomas Flamank and Michael Joseph memorial stone. They were leaders of the Cornish host who marched to London in 1497 to protest against taxes levied by King Henry VII. The stone was unveiled in May 1997 by Bodmin Town Mayor John Chapman and County Councillor Alastair Quinnell to mark the 500th anniversary of the Cornish rebellion.

Above: Exterior of the Wesleyan Chapel in Fore Street, prior to its re-building in 1880. Douglas Lewis collection.

Left: The interior of the Wesleyan Chapel was also re-modelled in the 1880s. Douglas Lewis collection.

Opposite above: The Passmore Edwards Free Library, designed by Silvanus Trevail, was founded in 1897 and was built on the site of the Western Inn. At one time, Bodmin Town Museum was located within the building. In this picture there seems to be a surfeit of policemen on duty. Perhaps someone of importance is about to 'hit town'.

Opposite below: This school in Robartes Road, opened in 1865 at a cost of £1,500 on land given by J.A. Robartes, had several names during its lifetime. These included Church School, National School, Bodmin Voluntary School and latterly St Petroc's Church of England Infants School. A popular teacher was Miss Ruth Betteridge, headmistress of the infant section. The school was demolished in the late 1980s/early 90s to make way for Bederkesa Court, a complex of flats for the elderly.

Once known as 'The New Inn' this popular watering hole is now known as 'The Cat and the Fiddle' public house, photographed here during a short period of closure in 2002. It has since re-opened much to the delight of its regular patrons.

The round building shown on the right of this picture of Bore Street, the ambulance station, was demolished in 1967. Around this time the nearby Bible Christian Chapel also closed, and the St John Ambulance Brigade subsequently took over those premises.

Town End in 1908. St Lawrence's Church, built in 1859 as the chapel for the County Asylum, is on the left among the trees. It was eventually sold by the Health Authority. The building is still in use and was re-roofed a few years ago. The Roman Catholic Priory building can be glimpsed on the right. The railings, like so many others, were removed during the Second World War.

Aerial view showing the nine-acre complex of St Lawrence's Hospital; Boundary Road is in the foreground.

Left: The Asylum Clock, a memorial to members of staff of the Cornwall Mental Hospital killed in the World Wars. The clock, designed by R.T. Buscombe of Bodmin and built on Corporation land, cost £200. It was unveiled in 1925 by J.C. Williams, Lord Lieutenant of Cornwall. The mayor, alderman J.A. Jago, and ex-mayor, W.A. Browning Lyne, and other dignitaries attended the ceremony. The committee responsible for the arrangements comprised J.B. Lewis, L. Berry, C. Weary, A. Weary and H.J. Whitehurst.

Below: Dating from 1906, this picture shows some of the workmen involved with the building of the Foster Hall. Work started in 1901, but was curtailed in November 1903 by the death of the architect, Sylvanus Trevail. Later the project was overseen by Mr John Kirkland. The hall was named after Mr Henry Durett Foster in recognition of his work for the institution.

Interior view of St Mary's Priory, which in June 1953 was elevated to abbey status, the first in the Lateran order since the reformation. The Rt Rev. Abbot General C.R.L. of Rome, head of the order throughout the world, and the Rt Rev. Abbot A. Smith of Hornsey, head of the Lateran order in England, headed an impressive roll call of Roman Catholic clergy. Abbot Aloysius Smith was enthroned by the Bishop of Plymouth, the Rt Rev. Francis Grimshaw, as the first abbot of Bodmin.

Dunmere was always a spot where Bodmin people could get away from it all. This group pictured in the early 1900s appear to be watching artists at work. The ladies are being quite adventurous in standing so close to the weir.

Above: The pond on the River Camel at Dunmere has always been a popular venue for swimmers. A hundred years ago, writers to the Cornish Guardian expressed concern about the safety aspect of this practice. Despite his brother having been drowned there, a Mr Sowden of Chatham in Kent wrote in support of the swimmers to say that Dunmere Pool was no more dangerous than any other river, and there was no whirlpool or hidden rocks.

Below: Dunmere Halt on the Southern Railway line to Wadebridge and Padstow.

Above: The Bodmin and Wenford railway is the second-oldest railway in the country. This picture shows a Beattie Tank locomotive working on a picturesque stretch of the line where it passes beside the River Camel near Dunmere Pool.

Below: This picture, postdated September 1906, shows the headmaster's residence at Harleigh School. The school was founded in 1874 by Mr John Stranger in Rhind Street and was moved in 1895. In 1905 it became known as Bodmin County School. Changes in the educational system meant changes of name and an influx of pupils. Later the school was again developed and afterwards offered a wider curriculum. It finally closed in December 1994.

The Duke of Cornwall's Light Infantry war memorial, popularly known as 'The Soldier Statue', outside the Victoria barracks entrance, was unveiled on 17 July 1924 by HRH the Prince of Wales, Duke of Cornwall (afterwards Edward VIII), as Colonel in Chief of the Regiment. The memorial, designed by L.S. Merrrifield and modelled by William Trigg, commemorates the 255 officers and more than 4,000 men of the Duke of Cornwall's Light Infantry killed in the Great War.

Opposite above: Today Bodmin is not quite devoid of steam locomotion. Here Green Arrow is pictured while on a special visit to the Bodmin and Wenford Railway in May 1999.

Opposite below: Old Bodmin General railway station buildings as they are today. The are now home to the Bodmin and Wenford Railway.

Before boarding for the journey to Bodmin Parkway, Douglas Lewis, a steam railway enthusiast, admires locomotive No. 60800, Green Arrow, which has just drawn into the old Bodmin General station, May 1999.

The busy sidings at the old Great Western Railway station as they appear today, thanks to a lively group of railway enthusiasts who are determined to keep steam locomotion alive in Bodmin.

Bodmin Southern Railway, known after nationalisation in 1948 as Bodmin North. The train is a 'down' to Wadebridge and Padstow. Today the site beyond the railway signal box and platform contains the Somerfield supermarket. Note the gaol tower in the background. Keith Weary collection.

Bodmin North, Southern Railway photographed at a quiet time between trains.

A deserted Bodmin North, Southern Railway station.

The imposing gateway to Bodmin Gaol looking very much as it always did, apart from a few modern 'adornments'. For many prisoners this was their last chance to glimpse the freedom of the outside world before facing up to the harsh gaol regime and possible execution.

Bodmin Gaol as it appeared in 1894. The civil part of the gaol was closed down in 1916, and the remainder closed in 1927. Since then the gaol has undergone several reincarnations. In the 1930s a Mr Lee from Norfolk purchased the complex and opened it to the general public. Admission was one shilling (5p) per head. Later a builder bought it for demolition and development, but this did not fully materialise. More recently it became a nightclub and also a tourist attraction owned by Terry and Denise Gilhooley.

A glimpse of the gaol complex from the garden of one of the nearby dwellings. One wonders what the occupants of the cottages thought of their neighbours.

Flaxmoor Terrace was at one time occupied by staff of the gaol. Some years afterwards No. 6 was purchased by Walter Bound who was later to become Alderman and mayor of Bodmin. Keith Weary collection.

Bodmin Gaol, showing the naval wing which was closed down in 1922. During the First World War, the Crown Jewels were secreted away in the depths of the gaol. Whether or not they were there during the Second World War remains one of Bodmin Gaol's enduring mysteries. What is certain is that during that war the gaol was used as the Civil Defence base and was also occupied for a time by American servicemen. Bodmin Library Collection.

The Old Laundry Building at Clerkenwater on the edge of Bodmin.

The old Bodmin Police Station in Pound lane as it looks today. It was once the Headquarters of the Cornwall Constabulary. The building was opened for business in 1867 and closed in May 1973 when the present day Police Station was opened.

TELEGRAMS: BOLT, BODMIN   TELEPHONE 32

ST. PETROC'S HOTEL, BODMIN
PROPRIETORS: W. P. AND E. L. BOLT

TWO TENNIS COURTS

RIDING HORSES KEPT — RIDING LESSONS GIVEN

The Georgian St Petroc's Hotel in St Nicholas Street, once the home of the Wallis family. According to the picture the hotel proprietors were Mr and Mrs Bolt. The establishment was one of the premier hotels in Bodmin. Later it became the South Western Electricity Board's district offices, which afterwards moved to Lostwithiel Road. Currently it is a residential home for the elderly.

ACCOMMODATION FOR TOURISTS

The Barley Sheaf
FAMILY & COMMERCIAL HOTEL

Proprietors:
R. & G. WEARY,
Fore Street,
Bodmin, Cornwall.

Tel.: 16

The Phoenix Restaurant run by Mrs Roy Weary. Patrons of this popular establishment, part of the 'Barley Sheaf' public house in Lower Bore Street, could always be sure of a real 'Bodmin' welcome and a good meal.

two

Bodmin People

Someone once said, 'You name it, someone in Bodmin has done it'. In all probability this is true. Bodmin people's achievements are legendary. Some were too early to be captured on film, others found fame or notoriety far away from Bodmin or Cornish soil. These include Thomas Flamank, Harry Dennison in Canada, John Belling, John Arnold, James Finn VC, Lt-Gen. Sir Walter Raleigh Gilbert ... the list could go on. This chapter is more about the ordinary people of Bodmin who have, each in their own quiet way, added to the rich mosaic of life in Cornwall's county town.

Above: Proud Bodmin campanologists display their bells outside St Petroc's Parish Church after restoration by Messrs Meare and Stainbank of London in 1910. Extensive work was also undertaken in the bell chamber at this time, supervised by Mr H. Barber. Among the ringers pictured are H. Pallot, Hugh King, Vicar W. Hender, W. Hosken, A.S.Collins, B.R.Lawrey, seated C. Couch and W.T.Verran.

Mrs Ruth Hobbs, now of Launceston, receiving a prize from Mayor Keith Searle for her entry in the Best Kept Garden in Bodmin competition in 1983–84. Also pictured are Mr Peter Borlase, head National Trust gardener at Lanhydrock, and Mrs Shirley Mewton.

Above: Street entertainer outside Arnold's Passage, off Fore Street.

Opposite right: The pomp of a civic procession as it makes its way up Fore Street in May 1952, after Alderman Horace Kinsman had been invested as mayor. Also shown is town clerk E.W. Gill. The old Palace Theatre is in the background.

Bodmin has a long tradition of carnival. This picture shows some of the participants in 1897 posing at St Lawrence's Hospital before moving off. T. Hambly, W. Bound, B. Kenny, J. Everett and F. Spear are shown.

Above: Carnival time is always eagerly awaited in Bodmin. Here the co-operative car takes the advantage to do a little advertising as the procession makes its way up Fore Street

Right: Portrait of Walter Bound (with 'comrades') when he was stationed at Lucknow, India. He sent this picture of himself as a greeting to his family in Bodmin in 1915. This portrait was taken by Omaid Singh and Sons, Sudder Bazaar, Lucknow, whose business was established in 1862, only a few years after the five-month-long seige of the British garrison ended.

Opposite below: Bodmin carnival-queen-choosing ceremony in the Priory Park, July 1948. Shown are Alderman A.G. Kinsman, mayor, and Mr Norman Lyne (speaking). Pictured is the carnival queen Miss Shirley Keenan, with her attendants. The fairy queen chosen on this occasion was Miss Carol Selly, seen here with her attendants.

Above: Walter Bound while serving with the DCLI. He was later to become mayor of Bodmin.

Right: Proud father Walter Bound with his daughter, who was later to become Mrs Roy Weary.

Mr Councillor Walter Bound
(THE MAYOR ELECT)
presents his Compliments and requests the pleasure of your company at the Reception at app. 1 p.m. in the Public Rooms following the Mayor Choosing on Monday, the 10th November.

The pleasure of the recipient can only be imagined, when in 1947 this invitation card dropped through their letter box from Councillor Walter Bound, mayor elect, inviting them to attend the mayor choosing ceremony.

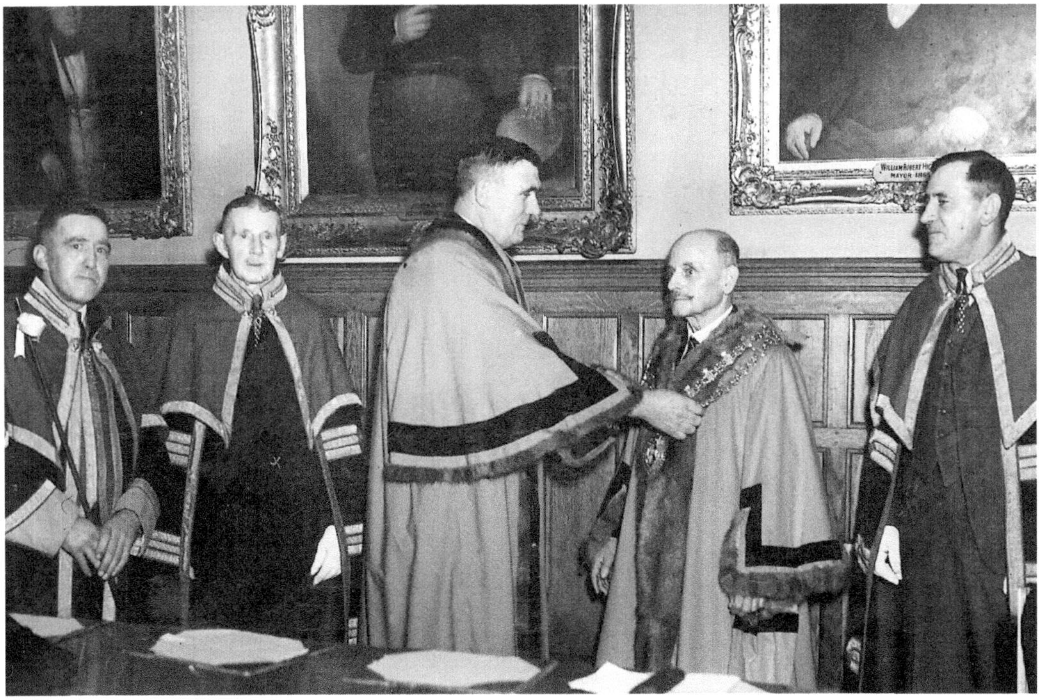

This picture shows Walter Bound being invested as mayor of Bodmin by Alderman Horace Kinsman at the mayor choosing ceremony in November 1947.

Above: Walter Bound chairing a council meeting soon after being invested as mayor of Bodmin in 1947. Mr E.W. Gill is clerk to the council. Also pictured is Councillor L.G. Hill. and Alderman H. Kinsman.

Left: The Bound family grave in the cemetery adjoining the Berry Tower. On one occasion during a town council meeting, Walter Bound found himself in the singular position of having a casting vote. He used it to good effect. His vote committed Bodmin Borough Council to purchase land at the Priory for a public park, a fact of which he was particularly proud and which is recorded on his grave memorial. The purchase was agreed at £8,000.

Right: A Clemens of Bodmin photograph showing two choirboys from St Petroc's Parish Church, Keith Weary and David Bound, incidentally both grandsons of Mayor Walter Bound.

Below: Celebrity entertainer and disc jockey Jimmy Savile, on a marathon walk from John o'Groats to Lands' End in March 1971, found time to visit the East Cornwall Hospital where he signed autographs and chatted to patients and staff. He was greeted on behalf of Bodmin by Mr R.G. Hedger, Mayor, at the Westberry Hotel. Also shown in this picture is Mr M. Cole, porter at the hospital.

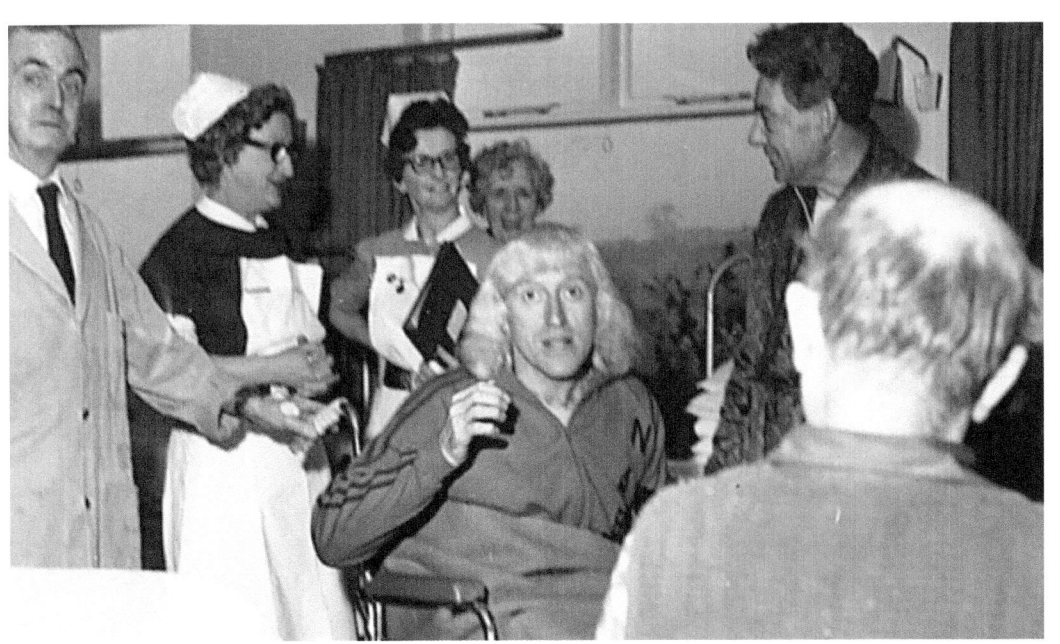

Beating the bounds at Bodmin in August 1972, Bodmin Mayor Councillor Thomas Hicks, is being 'bumped' by town clerk Ivor Whiting and A.F.J. Webb, borough surveyor, at Callywith Gate, at the start of the eighteen-mile route. Also shown are Dennis Taper, Eric Udy, Clive James, Gilbert Rawlings and town crier, Alfred Nicholas. James Riddle is holding the paddle bearing the Common Seal of the Borough carried aloft by the leader of the beat.

Beating the bounds. The crowd is scrambling for nearly minted coins hurled into the river at Blowing House by mayor Councillor T.J. Hicks. Among places on the route are Halgavor Bridge, Penbeagle Farm, Dunmere Bridge, Blowing House, Fletchers Bridge, St Lawrence and Laveddon.

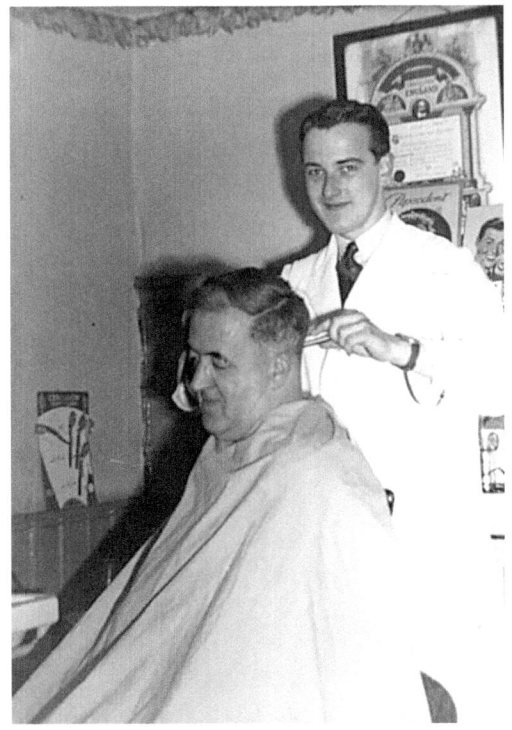

Above: The barrel organ party working in conjunction with Bodmin Carnival Committee to raise funds for St Lawrence's Hospital during the run up to the carnival in 1939. This picture shows Mrs Libby, Sue Carter, H. Taylor, Joan Tank, S. Stevens, Carrie Meagor and Mrs Trembath. Over £80 was raised by this sterling effort.

Right: This picture from 1948 shows Terance Weary while learning his trade with Mr Les Rowe at his barbershop in St Austell. Mr Weary was a well-known and popular Bodmin figure who ran his own hairdressing business in Higher Bore Street for many years. He was a great ambassador for, and promotor of, anything and everything to do with Bodmin.

Overleaf: Bodmin choir outing in 1913. Among those pictured are Miss Hardy, Miss Jewell, Miss Martin, Irwin Rowe, Vanderwolfe, junior Cicely Springett, L. Stevens and D. Stevens.

Above: August 1946 was a special time for the Bodmin Male Voice Choir. They made one of their several live radio broadcasts under the direction of Mrs Hearn. The Cornish Guardian tells that they sang with precision and clarity, with nigh perfect tone and diction, every word being distinct and audible. The choir were congratulated by the Mayor Alderman H.G. Kinsman. Mayoress Mrs Lilian Kinsman is in the centre of the picture.

Opposite above: Bodmin Male Voice Choir with Mrs Adelaide M. Hearn in 1934. Choir members shown are Reg Sloman, Hendy, Richardson, Gilchrist, Haskin, Burrows, W. Maker, Stevens and Mullis.

Opposite below: Bodmin Male Voice Choir under the conductorship of Mrs Hearn, pictured here in 1936. Mrs Hearn died in January 1955. The Cornish Guardian tells that her death was a great loss to the musical life of Bodmin.

Bodmin firemen pictured in 1906. Among those shown are firemen F. Weary, W. Shelley, J. Henderson, W. Solomon, H. Webster, bugler A. Tucker, Capt. Bawden, B. Gidley-Gerry (Hon. Surgeon), R.T. Buscombe, N. Climo, and G.B. Treverton (Hon. Sec.).

Above: This picture shows canvassing under way during the second election campaign in 1906 in the Bodmin Division, in which Thomas Agar Robartes threw his weight behind Mr Freeman-Thomas.

Right: Mr Freeman-Thomas, who contested the seat on behalf of the Liberal cause at a bye-election in July 1906. The result was Freeman-Thomas Liberal 4,969 and Sandys Tory 3,876.

Opposite left: Elections in the Bodmin Division were always fiercely contested. This picture shows Mr George Sandys, the prospective Unionist candidate, in the January 1906 election. He was later defeated by Thomas Agar Robartes. The Cornish Guardian heralded a Triumphant Liberal Victory and stated that Toryism was vanquished. Later the election result was disputed and Robartes was unseated, accusations of bribery, treating and undue influence having been made against him.

Opposite right: An elegant Mrs Sandys, wife of the defeated Unionist candidate.

Group of Great Western Railway staff and passengers posing for the camera at Bodmin Road railway station in 1905. Since 1984 the station has been known as Bodmin Parkway, but the old name lingers on in the hearts of many.

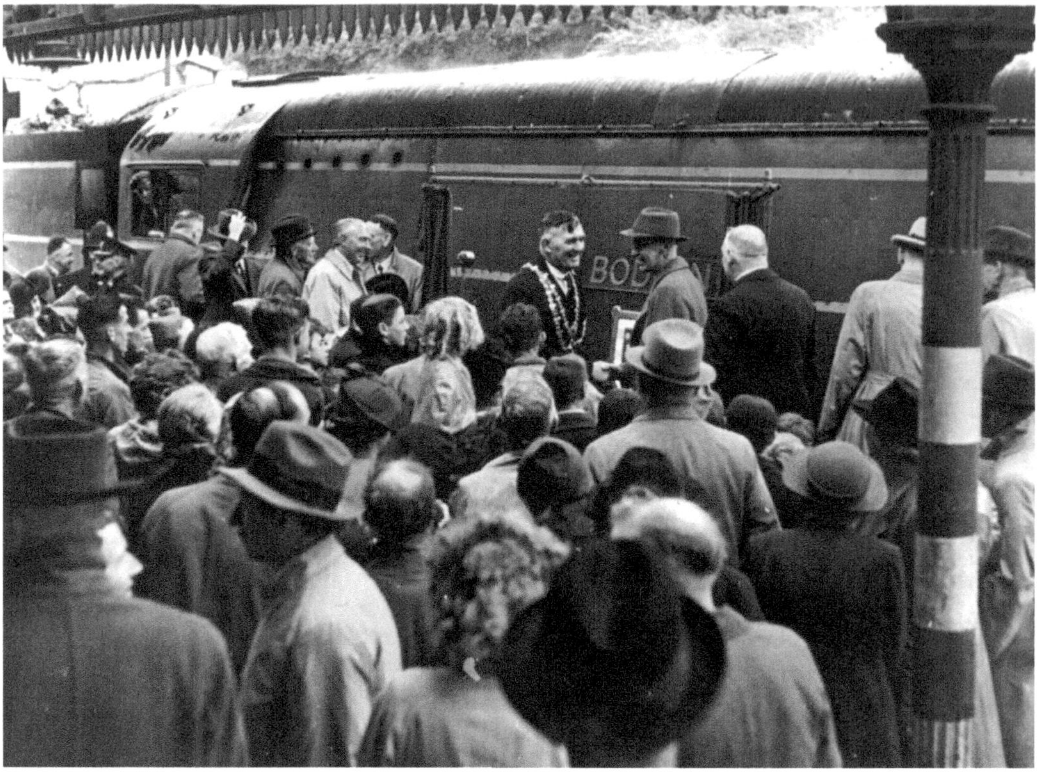

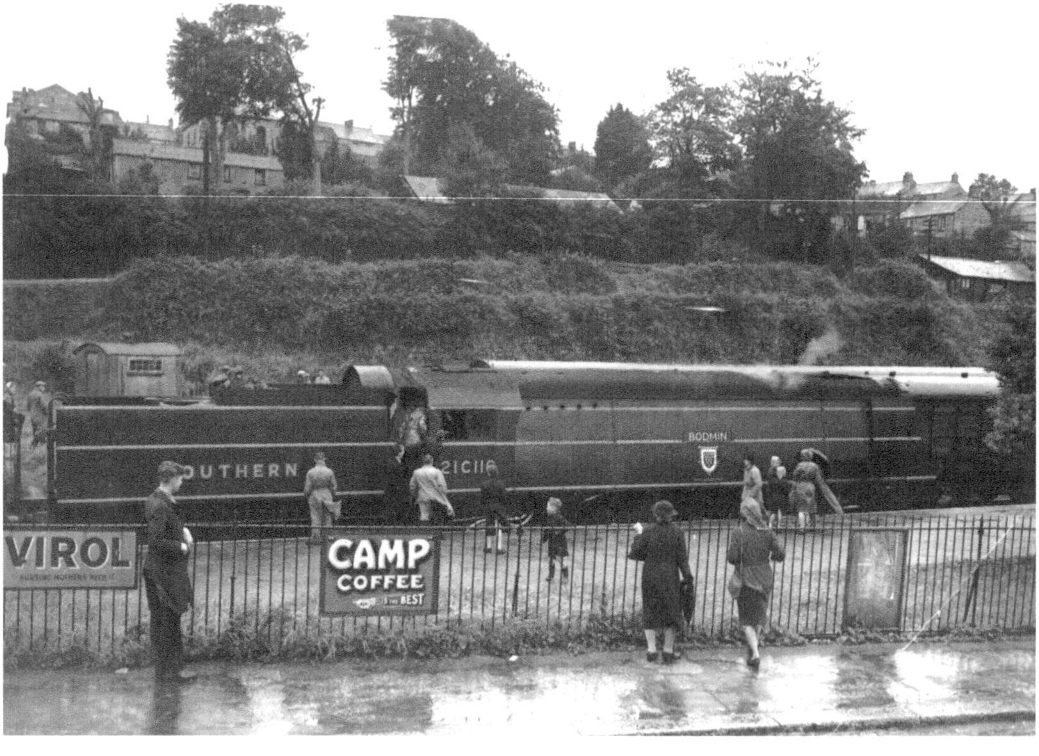
BODMIN
OUTHERN
21C116
VIROL
CAMP
COFFEE
BEST

Above: The strong arm of the law in force at Bodmin in early 1910. Experts will notice the subtle changes in uniform which took place in June that year. Numbers were transferred from breast to collar and sergeants' stripes were placed above the elbow.

Opposite above: A Southern Railway locomotive being named Bodmin by the mayor, Alderman H.G. Kinsman in August 1946. This picture shows the mayor greeting railway officials, including the chairman Col. Eric Gore Brown. Later the mayor donned the driver's cap and mounted the footplate. Town clerk Mr E.W. Gill stood on the step behind. Afterwards the mayor expressed his thanks to the railway company on behalf of Bodmin, the county town, as did other town dignitaries.

Opposite below: Southern Railway locomotive Bodmin being admired following the naming ceremony. These small boys must have felt that, with a locomotive named after their town, their dreams of becoming an engine driver had come one step nearer. At this time in 1946 Bodmin was the latest Westcountry class locomotive to be built out of the seventy planned by the Southern Railway.

The sheriff arriving on Mount Folly prior to attending the assizes in 1910.

Arrival of the sheriff at St Petroc's House in St Nicholas Street.

HRH Princess Chula Chakrabongse, Cornwall county commissioner of St John Ambulance Brigade, with Shirley Hamley and Rosemary Pooley, members of the Bodmin detachment, who are believed to be receiving awards.

St John Ambulance Brigade personnel on parade in Church Square probably on their way to church. Goss bicycle shop is in the background.

Bodmin has long enjoyed a thriving and successful tradition in every aspect of sport. This picture shows the tennis club in the early 1900s.

Above: A Bond photograph showing the Bodmin football team line-up with the club officials in 1920–21. Among those pictured are J. Burden, L. Brown, Mr Bowes, A. Weary, M. Rowe, G. Jane, C. Honey, H. Scantlebury, F. Vanderwolfe, F. Colwell, Mr Brewer, S. Roach and A. Thomas.

Opposite above: This photograph shows members of the Bodmin Girls Club in April 1906. Their theatrical production that year was called 'A Dress Rearsal' and was staged in the 'Church Institute'. Cast members included Millie Epinard, E. Tonkin, R. Spear, G. Salmon, H. Liddell, L. Burton and J. Coleman.

Opposite below: The finale cast of Dick Whittington staged by The Queer'uns Variety Company in the Public Rooms in 1948. Principal boy and girl were Pat Connor and Jean Goss respectively. Among others, shown are B. Dale, J. Dawe, A. Shelley, J. Ellery and J. Rowe. Who played the cat?

75

The cast of the nativity play performed in front of the high altar at St Petroc's Church at Christmas 1958. Among those shown are Keith Weary who played King Herod and Trevor Scantlebury who took the part of a shepherd.

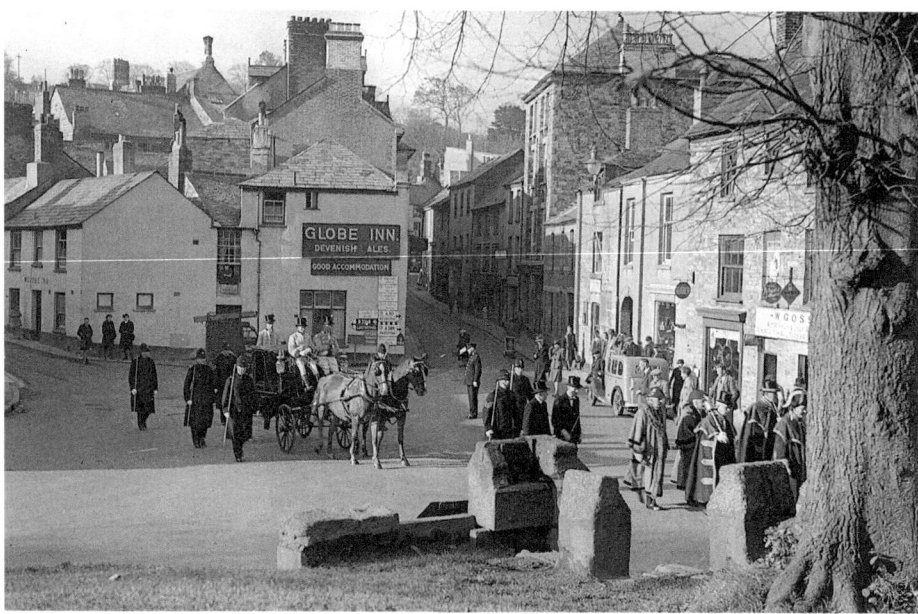

Despite all the disruption, hardship and uncertainty during the war years, life carried on and some things gave an air of stability and normality. In this picture from 1944, Judge McNaughton is being conveyed by coach across Church Square on his way to a service at St Petroc's Church escorted by the javelin men, prior to attending the assizes. The tall building on the right was the Fire Service Headquarters during the Second World War. The Globe Inn became The Duke of Cornwall Public House in the 1950s and was demolished in 1992.

three

Bodmin through war to peace

This section deals briefly with Bodmin during the years of the Second World War. Bodmin being a garrison town, there was a massive influx of troops to the Victoria Barracks. Evacuees also came, to escape the bombing of the big cities.

Local people were called upon to do their bit for the war effort. There was War Weapons Week, War Ships Week, a visit by the Princess Royal and a Salvage Drive. On the entertainment front there were dances and troop concerts in the Centenary Assembly Rooms. In February 1942 Polish officers gave a concert in the Public Rooms. In August that year, two German bombers swept over the town dropping bombs and firing machine guns, spreading terror and havoc. Several people lost their lives. Undoubtedly Bodmin people were shaken but picked themselves up, took stock and carried on with their daily lives.

Above: A familiar sight in Bodmin – the Duke of Cornwall's Light Infantry band marching down St Nicholas Street from the barracks in the early war years.

At the height of the Blitz on Plymouth in 1941 fire teams from several places, including Bodmin, were frequently called upon to assist their Devonshire counterparts. This picture shows R. Weary, Eric Benton, Monty Lobb, Les Symons, Charlie Wall and L. Stevens with colleagues in one of the Bodmin teams.

Just three of the many evacuees who came to Bodmin. In this picture, Peter and Paul, aged five and six years respectively, and John, who is obviously a little older, pose on the steps outside the Bodmin Centenary Chapel in July 1941. Where did they come from? Did anyone keep in touch after they returned home? Where are they now? Perhaps someone knows.

Everyone was called upon to do their bit on the home front. Bodmin women rose to the emergency. Here, in September 1941, housewives and young girls busy themselves making camouflage nets.

This picture, dating from October 1939, a month after war was declared, must have given Bodmin people a bit of a boost when it appeared in the local press. It shows part of the Bodmin Auxiliary Fire Brigade wearing their newly allocated protective clothing. Their new pumps are also on view.

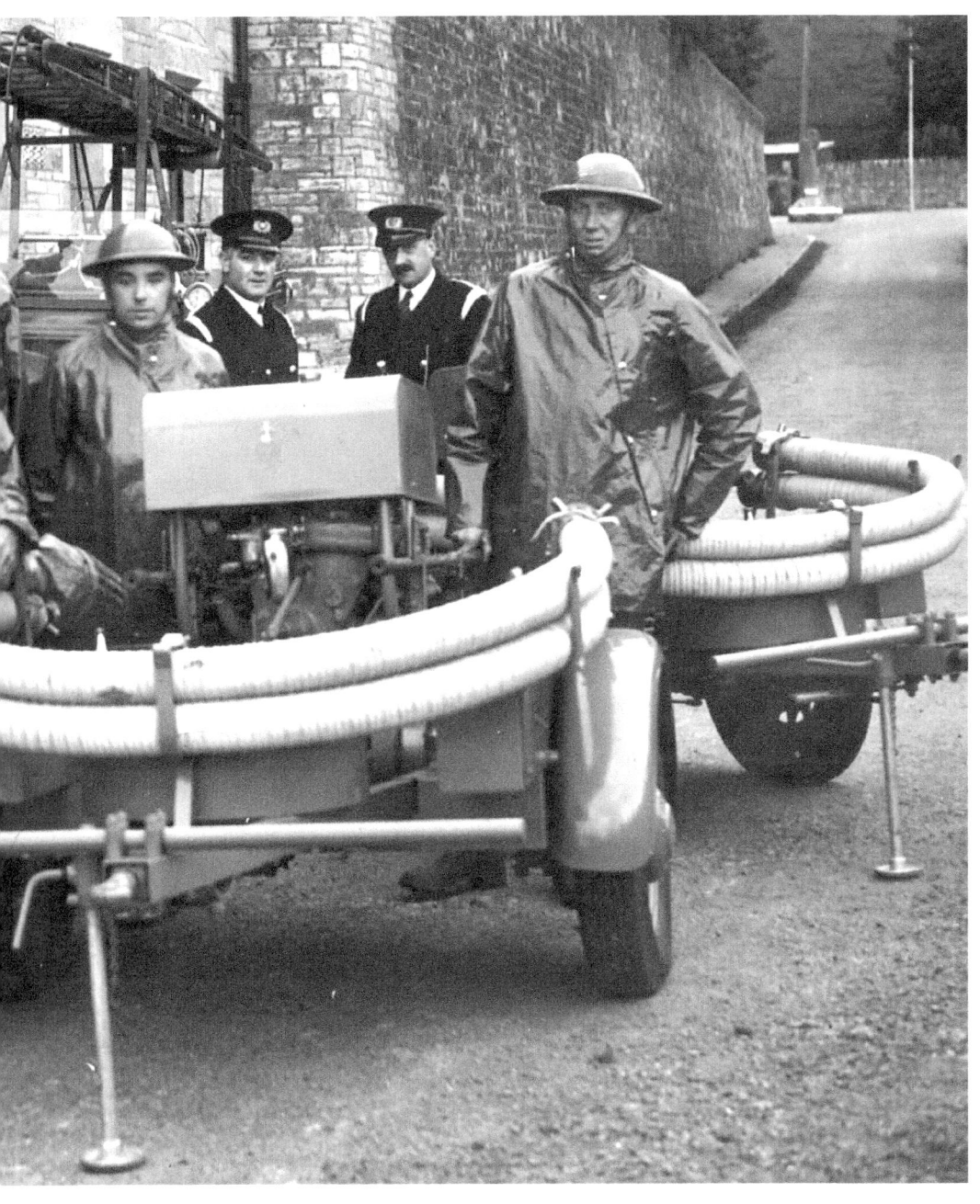

Roy Weary, a well-known commercial traveller, accomplished musician and landlord of the Barley Sheaf Public House in Lower Bore Street.

During the darkest days of the last war, entertainment was everything to lift morale. One of the top dance bands based in Bodmin was Roy Weary and the Down Beats, who had a huge regular following stretching from Newquay on the north coast across the county to Carlyon Bay on the south. In this picture Roy Weary is shown at the piano; he also played the accordian.

A morale boosting day for Bodmin: the Princess Royal as Commandant of the Auxiliary Territorial Service inspecting three companies of ATS while visiting units at Bodmin Barracks in July 1941. Also pictured is Lt.-Col. Mercer.

Roy Weary at the piano with a group of musicians from the Duke of Cornwall's Light Infantry, in full swing during a dance at the public rooms in the mid-1940s.

This picture shows War Weapons Week in May 1941. President of the week was Viscount Clifden. The event was opened by the Lord Lieutenant of Cornwall, E.H.W. Bolitho. Mrs B. Rathbone, the MP for the division also spoke. The Royal Marine band from Devonport, and ITC at Bodmin took part. All the fighting forces were represented, as well as the Civil Defence. The salute was taken at Town Wall. An indicator, near the Turret Clock, marked the funds rising daily total which was revealed by the mayor and town council members in turn.

War Ships Week, February 1942, was opened by Sir Charles Forbes, KCB, DSO, supported by the member for the division, Mrs B. Rathbone. Viscount Clifden was president for the week. Sir Charles took the salute at Town Wall. The aim was to raise £55,000 but in the event £64,731 13s 10d was raised. A 'design a poster and slogan competition' was held, and the winner was 'Lend the Navy your LSD and HMS it soon will be' was adjudged the best and came from Miss Daphne England.

Bodmin Borough Prisoner of War Fund fancy dress parade, August 1943. Organised by the British Legion, it attracted over 100 competitors and over £200 was raised. The judges were Misses J.A. Foster and A. Myers and Mesdames R. Williams and Carrol. Prize winners were Anne Scantlebury, Shirley Pomeroy, Frankie Harvey, Peter Fenne, Joyce Retallack and Dennis John. Apparently Bodmin needed to raise £364 a year to send 10 shilling weekly parcels to those from the town held prisoners of war.

The bomb-wrecked home of the Sargeant family in Mill Street after the air raid of August 1942. Army Rescue Squad members are propping up the building while other rescuers are trying to reach the trapped family underneath. Sadly eight members of the family were killed.

Rescue work continues apace despite the difficulties. There was no warning siren as the two German planes swooped onto the town, dropping 500lb bombs and firing machine guns. One leading firewoman, Miss Audrey Clark, stationed in Bodmin, well remembers being given an order by a top-flight fire officer to grab a car, collect his family, take them up onto the moor and stay there until the excitement was over.

This picture shows all that remained of the Primrose Dairy in Mill Street after the air raid in August 1942. Here, one employee, sixteen-year-old Edgar Tippett from Lanivet, was killed. Miss Irene Knight had a lucky escape as did Mr Douglas Davey, having left the premises for a few minutes. Two ladies standing nearby were blown up the garden path of a house but fortunately sustained little or no injury. Today the modern fire station occupies the site of the former gas works.

Pool Street littered with debris, August 1942. The bomb blast shattered plate-glass windows in the shops in Fore Street. Humour came through, however. One shop boasted on its emergency covering, 'we have no pains [sic], dear mother, now' while another stated, 'Draughty, yes; Windy, No'.

Burial service of the eight air raid victims who were interred in state at the cemetery. Five hearses took the victims to the cemetery. Soldiers based locally acted as bearers. The vicar, curate and Methodist minister officiated at the graveside. As a mark of respect the mayor and corporation attended with draped maces. Most businesses closed their doors at the time of the funerals.

This picture shows one of several Victory Arches mounted in Bodmin. This one stood at the junction of Mount Folly and Fore Street. Pictured are: L.G. Hill; F. Scantlebury and F. Burrows, mace bearers; Walter Bound, in top hat; town clerk E.W. Gill; Horace Kinsman, mayor; Mr F. Richards, the ex-mayor who served throughout the war years; S.M. Northey; S.T. Hore. The gentleman standing next to the mace bearer is believed to be Major Hare, Chief Constable of Cornwall. Northey's chemist shop is behind the police sergeant.

To celebrate both V-E Day and V-J Day, street parties were held all over Bodmin. This one in Corporation Terrace was no exception Among those pictured are Margaret Rowe, Esme Mullis, Rosemary Pender, Tony and Teddy Patterson, Mrs Mullis, Mrs Jenkins and Peter Hancock.

In August 1945 a service of thanksgiving for the return of peace was conducted in the Priory Park by the vicar Rev. R.A. Young and attended by the mayor and countless Bodmin people.

In July 1946 the Duke of Cornwall's Light Infantry had the Honorary Freedom of the Borough of Bodmin bestowed on the regiment. This picture shows Mayor H.G. Kinsman, with Mr E.W. Gill (town clerk), mace bearers Mr F. Scantlebury and Mr F. Burrows, and the town crier Mr S. Morris, on their way to the ceremony outside St Petroc's Parish Church.

Crowds gathered in Church Square on 1 July 1946 to witness the Honorary Freedom of the Borough of Bodmin granted to the Duke of Cornwall's Light Infantry Regiment, which had close associations with the town. The scroll was received by Gen. Sir Walter Venning. The regiment was later amalgamated with the Somerset Light Infantry and in 1959 the regimental flag was lowered for the last time.

The ties of friendship between the Duke of Cornwall's Light Infantry and Bodmin still continue today as is shown in this picture of the 4th/5th DCLI Old Comrades Association meeting at Bodmin in April 1992. Among those pictured are Bill Jago, Bert and Marjorie Tremain, Horace Vercoe, Rose Marks, George Johnson, Fred Hick, RSM Reg Philp, Frank Grigg (association secretary for fifty years), Cedric Ivey, Joe Kendall and Lennard Crocker.

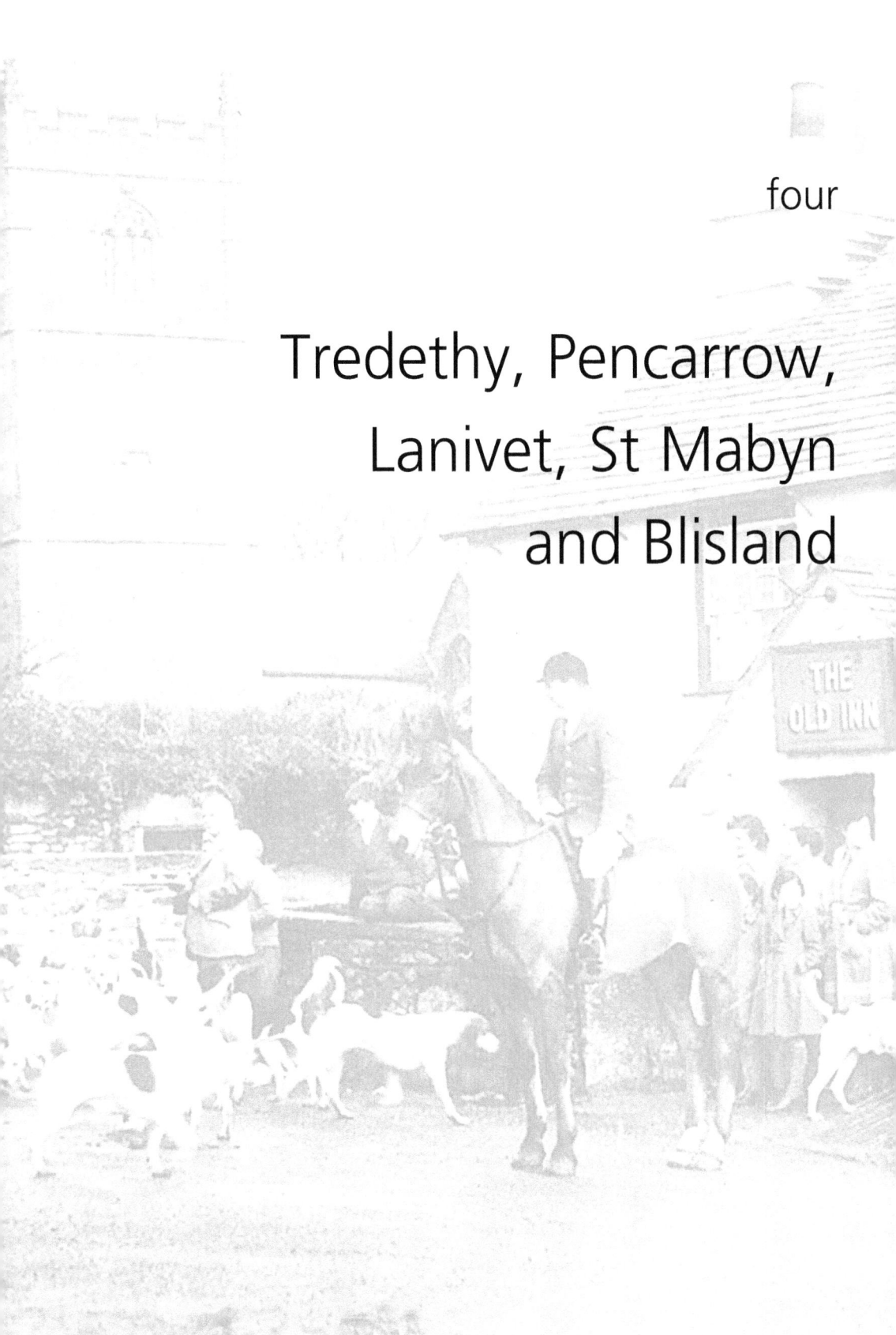

four

Tredethy, Pencarrow, Lanivet, St Mabyn and Blisland

This section explores one of the more diverse areas surrounding Bodmin, which includes Tredethy House with its Thai royal connection, the great house at Pencarrow, a giant granite curiosity and an interesting beam radio station.

A rare view of Tredethy House at Helland under snow in 1947, the year of the great blizzard. The house, dating from the sixteenth and seventeenth centuries, was the seat of the May, Lang and Hext families. During the Second World War, Tredethy House was turned into a hostel, and later became the Cornish home of Prince Chula and Princess Elizabeth of Thailand. In 1955 Prince Chula offered Tredethy to the Cornwall St John Ambulance Brigade for use as a county headquarters in wartime. The offer was accepted by the Civil Defence Authorities. Following the deaths of Prince Chula in 1964 and Princess Elizabeth in 1971, Tredethy came up for sale, with an asking price of £65,000. Today it is a private hotel. Local people still recall seeing the Royal Standard flying over the house.

Who in 1947 received this individual Christmas greeting from Prince and Princess Birabongse? The greeting is written in green ink and reads, 'We have just returned from America and found your Christmas card waiting for us… We thank you very much for your good wishes which we heartily reciprocate… and how's the Launceston ghost? The card was simply signed – Bira. Prince Bira, a cousin of Prince Chula, with his car sporting Thai racing blue was well known in motor racing circles.

St Mabyn Church, dating from the fifteenth century is dedicated to St Mabena. The first incumbant was instituted in 1267. Stained-glass windows commemorate members of the Hext, Barratt and Andrew families. The church tower gargoyles showing birds and animals are interesting.

Fore street, St Mabyn, probably in the 1930s before developers had begun to eye up small country villages. Today an old enamel Automobile Association sign on the seventeenth-century St Mabyn Inn tells us that the village is 'exactly' 234H miles from London. Who were the two small boys? Whose was the delivery van?

This picture shows a meet of the North Cornwall Fox Hounds outside the Old Inn at St Breward. A scene to be cherished as the continuance of this age-old country pursuit is under serious threat.

Fox hunting, shooting and fishing have long been a part of life on and around Bodmin Moor. This scene, captured by George Ellis, shows the North Cornwall Fox Hounds about to move off from Gam Bridge, St Breward.

Picture postcard view of Blisland Church, the main fabric of which dates from Norman times. The church is dedicated to two brothers, St Protus and St Hyacinth. Over the decades the former name has been corrupted to the more parochial St Pratt. The church, close to the village green, one of few in Cornwall, is full of interesting features.

Members of Launceston Old Cornwall Society visiting Jubilee Rock, Pendrift Common, Blisland, in the early 1970s. The giant rock is carved with numerous symbols depicting the royal coat of arms, commerce, industry, agriculture, plenty and Britannia, to mark the golden jubilee of King George III. They are the work of Lt. John Rogers and a recruiting party of the 65th Regiment who visited the village in October 1810. The carvings of Queen Victoria are newer.

Pencarrow House, Washaway, designed by Robert Allanson. Building began in 1760 and Pencarrow has been in the Molesworth St Aubyn family since that time. A mile-long drive, edged with rhododendrons, camellias, and other shrubs, planted by Sir William Molesworth, Bt, MP, during parliamentary recesses in the mid-nineteenth century brings the visitor to Pencarrow House. Sir Arthur Sullivan, a close friend of the family, wrote the music for *Iolanthe* while staying here in 1882. Since the 1970s the gardens have undergone an extensive replanting programme. Today, Pencarrow is also famed for 'Snowdrop Sunday' an early spring attraction when the sight of carpets of snowdrops is enjoyed by many visitors.

St Benet's Abbey, founded in 1411 as a Benedictine hospital or Lazar house at Lanivet. It was built on land belonging to Giffard, the lord of the manor. In the mid-sixteenth century, under the Chantry Act, it was seized by the Crown and described in old documents as the 'House called St Benet's' belonging to the churchwardens. At the Dissolution it came into the hands of the Courtenay family who sold the property in 1710. It was purchased by a Mr Bernard Pennington who afterwards sold it to a Mr Grose. Later the property was converted into a residence and today it is a hotel and restaurant.

Bodmin Beam radio station near Lanivet was opened in October 1926 by Bodmin's mayor, Arthur Browning Lyne, who sent the first message. At Christmas 1927 it sent 140,000 words a day, this daily figure had risen to 180,000 by the following year. At the outset of the Second World War the site was vacated and temporarily closed, but it was re-opened in 1940 and leased to the Air Ministry and RAF. In 1947, control passed to Cable and Wireless and it was extensively used by the Admiralty. In March 2002, after a 75-year history, the station closed.

The Sealed Knot Society pictured during the re-enactment of a battle in the grounds of Pencarrow in 1988. The society originated in the seventeenth century as a secret society dedicated to the restoration of Charles II. In this picture, the skirmish is reaching its height as the opposing forces strive to get the upper hand.

Great granite slabs obviously hauled from a local quarry form the picturesque Delphy bridge over the River De Lank between St Breward and Blisand.

five

Lanhydrock, Respryn and Carminnow Cross

This section focuses on the eastern side of Bodmin showing the great house of Lanhydrock, the bridge at Respryn, and Carminnow Cross, one of the antiquities of the area.

Above: A postcard scene of Lanhydrock and St Hydroc's Church dated May 1914. Originally Lanhydrock belonged to the Augustinian Priory at Bodmin. At the Dissolution it came into the Glynn family and afterwards Lyttleton and Trenance. In 1620 it was purchased by Sir Richard Robartes, a merchant banker from Truro. The Robartes family gave the property to the National Trust in 1953. Miss Everilda Robartes, who died in 1969, was the last family member to live at Lanhydrock.

Above: One of the jewels of Lanhydrock, shown on this postcard, is the 116-feet long Jacobean Gallery, which stretches the length of the north wing. The barrel-vaulted ceiling is remarkable for its craftsmanship. Its plasterwork is 24 star-shaped panels portraying Old Testament subjects, with smaller panels showing real and fabulous birds and animals.

Below: This picture shows the picturesque Respryn Bridge spanning the River Fowey near Lanhydrock. In 1947, the eminent Cornish artist J. Lamorna Birch painted a pair of pictures, of Respryn and of Horsebridge on the River Tamar. Later the canvases were exhibited all over Cornwall and afterwards presented to HRH Princess Elizabeth as a wedding gift from the Duchy.

Opposite below: The ornate two-storeyed gatehouse at Lanhydrock was started by John Lord Robartes in 1636 but not completed until 1651. In 1881 the house was extensively damaged by fire. Luckily the entrance porch and north wing remained intact. Lady Juliana Robartes was gravely affected by the disaster and died within a few days. Lord Robartes died the following March. Later, Charles Robartes, the new Viscount Clifden, rebuilt the house we see today.

The Halfway House in the Glynn valley, pictured in the 1930s, long before the ever-growing volume of traffic necessitated the widening of the bridge and alterations to the roadway. In recent years the inn was severely damaged by fire and has since been rebuilt.

This elderly gentleman is obviously out for an afternoon stroll and has taken a moment to survey the rolling countryside near Carminnow Cross or 'Carminnon' Cross, 1H miles from the centre of Bodmin. It once marked the boundary between the parishes of Bodmin, Lanhydrock and Cardinham. When work started on the Bodmin bypass in 1975, the cross, one of the finest in Cornwall, was moved and later re-sited in the centre of a new traffic roundabout.

six

Altarnun, Five Lanes, Trewint and North Hill

This section centres on two parishes, and the villages, hamlets and people in them; as well as the sports, crafts, celebrations and traditions which made them what they were and helped them to cling on to their identities.

Above: A lone horseman contemplates the upper reaches of the river Fowey as it courses the desolate stretches of Bodmin Moor. The scene, under wide-open skies, with scarcely a habitation in sight, emphasises just how lonely the moor can be.

Above: Who was this moorland shepherd leading his flock home across the desolate moor near the foot of Roughtor?

Below: A rutted track heading to the half-mile long, rocky-crested summit of Kilmar Tor, on the eastern flank of Bodmin Moor. At one time a railway line crossed the vast expanse to serve the granite quarry on Kilmar.

Opposite below: These men are busy cutting turf for fuel near the foot of Roughtor, in 1908. Roughtor is Cornwall's second-highest point, shown here with a view toward Brown Willy. Today turf cutting has almost vanished from the moorland scene. Fortunately the old craft is kept alive by one or two familes who have long lived and enjoyed the moorland way of life.

Altarnun village soon after the war memorial, a rough hewn granite Celtic cross, was unveiled by Mrs Kittow of Tredaule in March 1920. Many parishioners witnessed the ceremony. The service was conducted by the vicar, the Rev. A.H. Thorold, assisted by the Wesleyan minister Rev. W.L. Bennett and the Rev. R.R. Tregunna. Mr J. Climo was chairman of the memorial committee. The long-gone ford through the Penpont Water was off to the right of the picture.

A view of Altarnun on 24 May 1950 on the occasion of the opening of Wesley Cottage at Trewint. A special evensong service, emphasising ecumenical spirit, was conducted by the Rev. W.A. Kneebone, during which a number of hymns penned by Wesley were sung.

Altarnun village. Part of the barn building in the centre of the picture has been converted. At one time Frank Hamley had a cobbler's shop here. He was also a part-time postman; with a postal delivery walk which took him all around the parish and to the remote moorland farms. The six properties pictured were once sold for £12,000.

Interior of Altarnun Church, known as 'The Cathedral of the Cornish Moors', showing the magnificent rood screen, Norman granite font and the array of fifteenth-century wooden bench ends.

Penpont, Altarnun, as it looked in the 1940s. This was birthplace of one of Altarnun's celebrated sons, Nevil Northey Burnard. Burnard went to London and became a famous sculptor. Later he took to drink, returned to Cornwall and died a pauper in Redruth workhouse. The plaque on the frontage of Penpont was positioned by the Launceston Old Cornwall Society in 1950. At one time the nearby 'Maid Marian' store was the Ring O'Bells inn. Later it became a private dwelling, before becoming a shop in 1966.

Altarnun post office, which closed in 2002 but quickly re-opened in alternative premises before the start of the Christmas postal rush. Who today remembers Mr Smith, postmaster in the village for many years?

Main Street, Altarnun, as it looked in the 1970s, when Annie Williams kept her grocery shop there. Mr Williams repaired boots and shoes in a nearby premises. Affectionately remembered is Pooley's Grocery and General Store. The Pooley family sold the business in August 1986 and it finally closed some years later.

Altarnun school group. Among those pupils pictured are Clare Hardy, Garfield Jasper, Margaret Whale, Peter Retallack and Brian Retallack. The teacher is Mrs Rowe.

Altarnun held its first carnival in 1948 and it soon became the highlight of the village year. It was counted a great honour among local girls to be chosen carnival queen – a title which, in that first year, went to Megan Mutton, followed the next year by Jean Terry. In this picture from 1950 the carnival queen is Dolly Smale, pictured with her attendants Margaret Smith, Sylvia Jasper, Eileen Jasper and Thelma Warring. Sadly, Altarnun's carnival tradition ceased in the late 1990s.

Altarnun has always prided itself on fielding one of the best football teams in the district. Among those shown in this mid-1940s line-up are Bob Roberts, Gordon Williams, John Davey, Charles Dawe, Charles Smith, Leonard Neale, Bill Retallack, Dick Jasper and the three Willcocks brothers Gordon, Norman and Fred.

The Kings Head Hotel at Five Lanes is shown in the centre of this old view. The clutch of buildings on the right have been demolished to make way for the car park. The rounded corner-wall has gone, behind which stood the village pump; the site is now occupied by a bungalow. Once Five Lanes held a thriving regular market for the sale of cattle, sheep, horses and ponies, but this closed down in August 1990. Today, modern housing developments cover much of the area.

Five Lanes as it used to be. This was the travellers' view when entering the village from Launceston. The wooden house on the left has gone, as has the old blacksmith's shop on the right. Alec Scott's garage was demolished about fifty years ago.

Another corner of Five Lanes, shown in a view from the early 1900s, before the village had two bypasses. The original A30 effectively cut the village in two; then came the relief road which took traffic away from the village. Today the main A30 trunk road has been upgraded and passes the village on a flyover. The blacksmith's shop on the left with the sign was Williams, and almost opposite was a second such premises, Rowe. Mutton's shop was on the right and Scott's garage on the left.

Soon after their formation in the early 1970s, the Trigg Morris Men made a visit to Five Lanes as part of their Easter Monday county-length tour. Here the team are shown strutting their paces outside the Kings Head Hotel.

Wesley Cottage in Duck Street, Trewint, saved from demolition and afterwards restored by the Methodists of the North Hill circuit, shown here on dedication day, 24 May 1950. John Wesley was taken in by Digory and Elizabeth Isbell when he called on them in April 1744; and during the ceremony the door was unlocked by their great-great-great-grandson, Mr Thomas Isbell of Manchester, using the same key that had been used by his ancestors.

Mr Roy Neale, stone-hedging at Trewint. He built the Pilgrims Garden wall opposite Wesley Cottage in 1958. Mr Neale is well known for his craftsmanship over a wide area and has won many trophies in competition.

Above: The wild Bodmin Moor landscape is punctuated by old granite-built slate-clad farmsteads. Trederris at Altarnun is typical. This is how it looked in the late 1980s.

Below: View toward Sharp Tor, one of the smallest of the numerous Bodmin Moor tors, in an area named Twelve Men's Moor. The tiny village of Henwood is tucked into a crease in the landscape.

Right: St Torney's Church at North Hill, noted for the fine memorials to the Spoure and Vincent families. The old slate tombstone that remembers Arthur Peter, who died in 1828, was once in the churchyard and was carved by Nevil Northey Burnard. It is now in the church porch. The stone was repositioned in conjunction with Launceston Old Cornwall Society.

Below: In 1810, North Hill Wesleyan Chapel, shown in this picture, was opened for public worship, after a Mr Jasper advanced the money for the building. The dedicatory sermon was preached by the Rev. John Riles, chairman of the district. Among the early trustees were Messrs E. Jasper, T. Jasper, Samuel Peter, W. Pearce, Edward Brown and Matthew Wevill. This chapel soon became the mother of others in the district, including those at Coads Green and Bathpool.

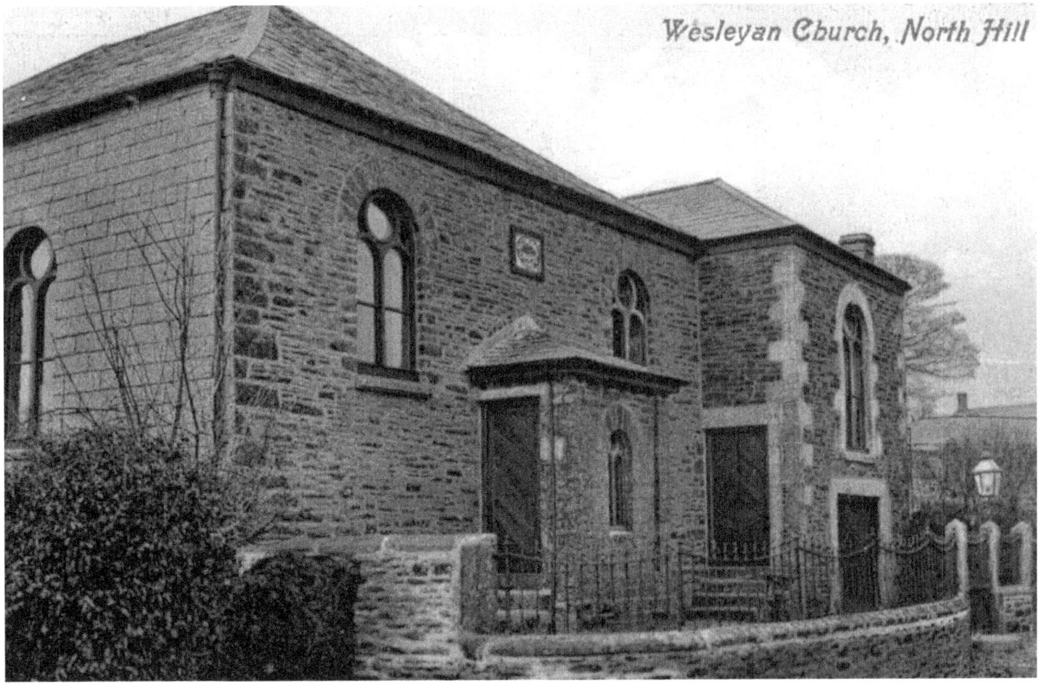

A meet of the Bolventor Harriers at Berrio Bridge on the river Lynher was always awaited with anticipation by local people. No banner waving by protesters or questions being asked in the Houses of Parliament or threats of a possible fox hunting ban in those times.

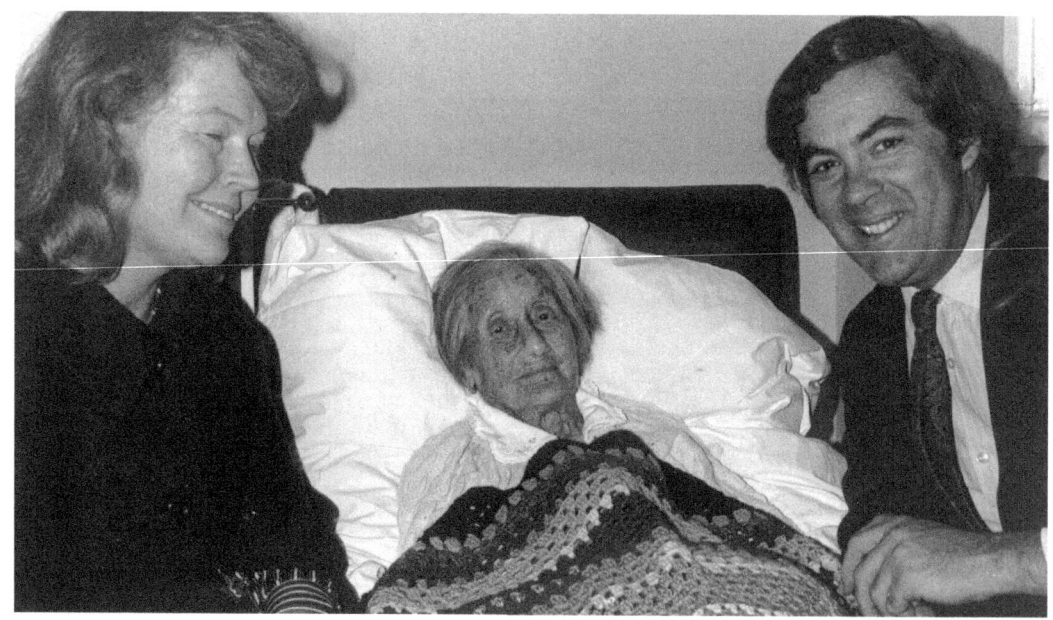

Mrs Lilias Browning Williams celebrating her 108th birthday at St Mary's Hospital in Launceston in 1976. Pictured are Joy and John Pardoe, Liberal MP for North Cornwall (1966–79). Mrs Williams was always a keen supporter of the Liberal party. Apart from relatives, John Pardoe was Mrs Williams' favourite man, closely followed by John Doyle of Westward Television fame. Mrs Williams was the oldest member of the Ancient Order of Foresters and chief ranger of Devon and Cornwall United District. Mrs Williams was born in Camelford in November 1868 and died in St Mary's Hospital Launceston Feb 12th 1979 aged 110 years.

seven

Bolventor, Jamaica Inn, Dozmary Pool and Davidstow

This section features the heart of Bodmin Moor, the famous Jamaica Inn, Bolventor village as it was over eighty years ago, the dark mystic waters of Dozmary Pool, and Davidstow.

Above: A 1919 view from Deep Hedges by Bolventor Church, where the old A30 trunk road swooped up to the village and Jamaica Inn. Shown on the right is Bolventor National School built in 1846. Its replacement opened in 1878 and closed after 114 years in 1992, due to dwindling pupil numbers. The last pupil was Tina Hooper. Bolventor post office, kept for a number of years by Mr and Mrs Frank Sleep, was one of the buildings in the foreground.

Left: The welcome sign of Jamaica Inn facing the old A30 trunk road at Bolventor, pictured here by Charles Woolf of Newquay. The sign was replaced around 1991. Today visitors are brought to the hostelry by a slight diversion from the newer dual carriageway which passes behind Jamaica Inn. The trunk route was opened by government minister Christopher Chope.

Jamaica Inn, immortalised in 1936 by Daphne du Maurier's famous romantic novel. At one time the hostelry belonged to the novelist Alistair Maclean. The two small boys pictured are Billy Winn and David Sleep. The war memorial occupies its original position. Older villagers still remember postman Arthur Reddicliffe, and Mr and Mrs Couch and Mrs Emma Nottle, who ran two small shops in nearby Jamaica Inn Cottages.

As this picture shows, motorists are beginning to discover Jamaica Inn. Once, the inn was a mecca for moorland people and it held a full licence until 1905. Later it became a Temperance House. In 1948 Launceston County magistrates refused a full licence application for Jamaica Inn from Mr Stanley Thomas of Plymouth. Opposition came from publicans in the area who believed they could meet all demands. Today Jamaica Inn is a fully fledged public house.

Diminutive Bolventor Church, closed for many years, faces an uncertain future as it has recently become the centre-piece of a wrangle between the church authorities, local people and developers.

Dozmary Pool is a large natural lake on Bodmin Moor. Legend has it that King Arthur threw his sword Excalibur into the waters. Until 1900 the lake was reputed to be bottomless, but a severe drought proved differently. As this picture from 1931 shows, St Luke's Chapel Sunday School scholars held their annual anniversary 'tea treats' by the pool and there was boating for everyone, with the boat and boatman being hired from Looe.

By the looks on these faces in 1966, boating on Dozmary Pool as part of the St Luke's Sunday School anniversary celebrations was enjoyable and hundreds of people from a wide area still attended the services. Formerly, everything from tea-urns to seating, even ice-cream and squash, had to be transported to the lakeside by horse and cart, but by 1966 a tractor was in attendance. Sadly the tea-treats no longer take place and at the time of writing, May 2003, the future of St Luke's Chapel hangs in the balance.

This family group are enjoying a well-deserved breather after 'making it' to the top of Brown Willy, Cornwall's highest point, in September 1988. Shown are Arthur, Barbara, Steven and Stuart Masters, and Dorothy, Ian and Andew Neale. Sadly the letterbox on the summit has disappeared.

Davidstow Church boasting its fifteenth-century tower, which during the Second World War was a navigational landmark for aircraft approaching the nearby airfield. Inside the church there is an interesting display of bench ends. Charlotte Dymond, murdered at Roughtor Ford in the nineteenth century, is buried in the graveyard.

One of several reminders that part of Davidstow Moor became an RAF station from October 1942. At an altitude of 970 feet above sea level, 370 acres of moorland and some farms were requisitioned. Fog was a curse for planes taking off and landing. One pilot based for a short time at Davidstow, Mr Nigel Newton, recalls that visibility on the airfield was often so bad that everything was 'fogged out', making flying impossible. Today the Moorland Flying Club use some of the old buildings. At the time of writing this book, the old runways are being removed for afforestation.

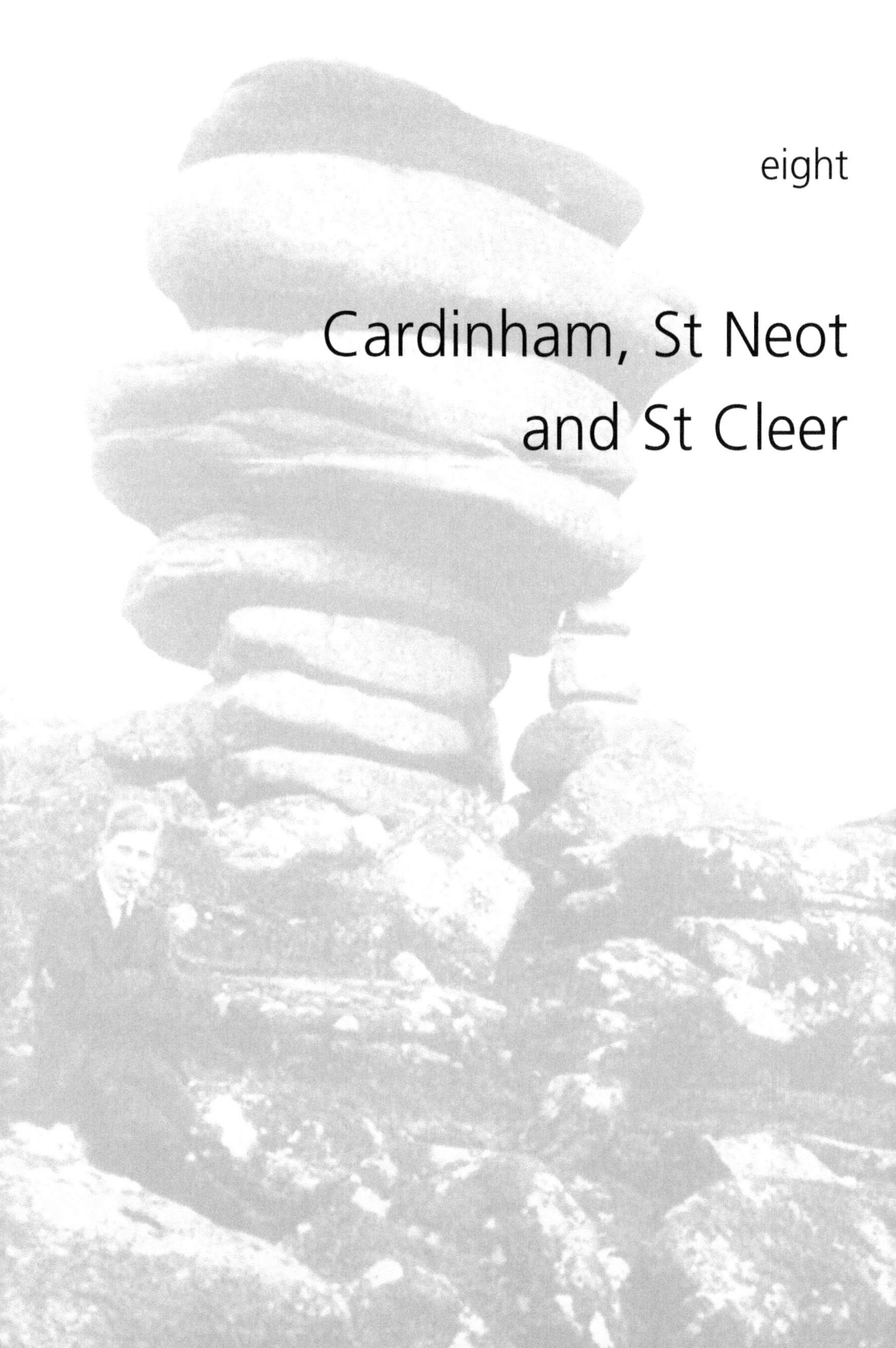

eight

Cardinham, St Neot and St Cleer

This section centres on three parishes on the part of Bodmin Moor which seems to get squeezed as two main arterial roads, the A30 and A38, which are never far away, begin to converge on Bodmin.

Above: This old postcard shows granite-built fifteenth-century St Meubred's Church at Cardinham, focal point of the 9,500-acre parish. The three-stage church tower hosts eight bells and the clock is a memorial to those parishioners who perished in the Great War. There are nearly seventy carved wooden bench ends dating from the fifteenth to sixteenth centuries and a Norman font. Visible to the right of the steps in this view is the magnificent ninth-century Cornish granite cross.

Below left: Laurie Smith, a Hampshire man who became in turn a soldier, sailor, bank robber, hobo and leather worker, which craft he learnt from a fellow convict while doing time in a Canadian gaol. At Moor Cottage, Cardinham, Laurie tooled handcrafted leather belts, keyrings and handbags, all delicately carved with flowers, plants, birds and his trademark toadstool. A favourite subject on larger items was a team of shire horses ploughing.

Below: Medieval leatherwork vessels also fascinated Laurie Smith, who made quiver bags, black jacks, costrols and cavalry bottles. This photograph shows a leather bombard, a ten-gallon water-carrying vessel. One was presented to the Canadian High Commissioner and another can be admired in Westminster Abbey.

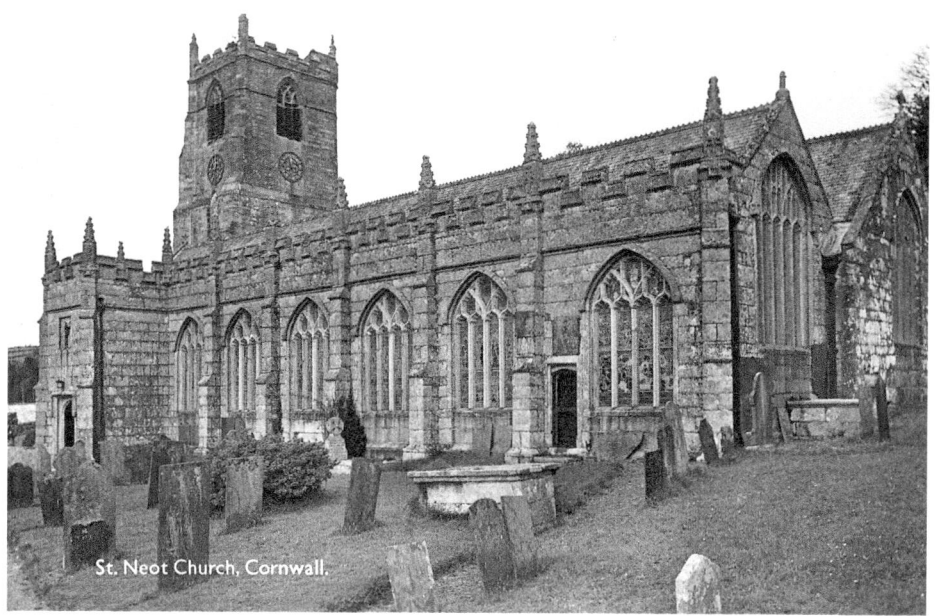

St Neot Church, probably one of the most visited churches in Cornwall. To mark the escape of Charles II after the battle of Worcester by hiding in an oak tree, an oak branch is hoisted to the top of the church tower annually on 29 May, Oak Apple Day. It remains in full view from the ground until the following year, so keeping alive a Royalist tradition by request of a seventeenth-century parishioner.

Looking down from Goonzion Downs on to St Neot village, tucked away in a pleasant wooded valleycoursed by a tributary of the River Fowey. The village continues to grow but is still arguably one of the more picturesque villages on the southern side of Bodmin Moor.

Left: Some of the glory of St Cleer Church has been lost, the building having been heavily restored in the thirteenth century. The three-stage tower is 97 feet high; the wagon roof is original. In 1904 a major restoration took place when ancient box pews were removed. Fortunately the range of seventeenth-century text boards, unique in Cornwall, remain. There are monuments to several important local families.

Right: Nonagenarian Wilfred Hoskin is one of St Cleer's grand 'old' characters. A passionate lifelong sportsman, he played football for Plymouth Argyll, for Torquay United and for almost every team in the Liskeard area; he also played cricket. Today he plays snooker, winning numerous prizes, cups, shields and medals. His other interest is studying the local history of his patch of Bodmin Moor.

Left: Pearl Olver was St Cleer's 'Queen of the May' in 1946. Among those shown are Betty Brokenshire, Elsie Sherman, Shirley Hambly, Zena Bradshaw, Shirley Hoskin and Ann Webster. Two boys, Brian Wills and Brian Riddle, collected primroses.

Above: Railway Terrace in St Cleer, pictured as it was in 1914. It was originally a collection of small cottages built to house miners and railway workers employed around Caradon Hill. The horseman is Dr Smale from Pensilva, 'doing his rounds'. He also had a surgery in Railway Terrace. Today Railway Terrace is more often called Darite. Exactly when the old name began to lose favour is something of a mystery, but Wilfred Hoskin distinctly remembers both names being used in tandem nearly ninety years ago.

Below: During the dark uncertain days of the Second World War, when invasion by German forces from across the English Channel was a serious threat, every village had its own 'Captain Mainwaring and Dad's Army' contingent, ready to repel enemy troops. This picture shows part of the St Cleer Home Guard in the 1940s.

The famous wind-carved granite outcrop of the Cheesewring, pictured in the early 1900s. Today it is teetering near the quarry edge on Stowe's Hill. Who is the man enjoying the view?

Dreynes bridge, spanning the upper reaches of the River Fowey. The plaque on the bridge is dated 1876. Today the scene is drastically altered. The river bank on one side is lined by huge beech trees and the area is a nature reserve.